The Problem with Masturbation

It's All About Me

Winston T. Smith

New Growth Press

www.newgrowthpress.com

New Growth Press, Greensboro, NC 27404
Copyright © 2009 by Christian Counseling & Educational
Foundation. All rights reserved. Published 2009.

Cover Design: The DesignWorks Group, Nate Salciccioli and
Jeff Miller, www.thedesignworksgroup.com

Typesetting: Robin Black, www.blackbirdcreative.biz

ISBN-10: 1-934885-96-7
ISBN-13: 978-1-934885-96-3

Library of Congress Cataloging-in-Publication Data

Smith, Winston T., 1966-
 The problem with masturbation: It's all about me   / Winston
Teal Smith.
    p. cm. -- (Resources for personal change)
 Includes bibliographical references and index.
 ISBN-13: 978-1-934885-96-3 (alk. paper)
 ISBN-10: 1-934885-96-7 (alk. paper)
 1. Masturbation--Religious aspects--Christianity. 2. Sexual
fantasies. 3. Sex--Religious aspects--Christianity. I. Title.
 BT708.5.S65 2009
 241'.66--dc22

                                2009006864

Printed in Canada
20 19 18 17 16 15 14 13   7 8 9 10 11

t's normal; everybody does it."

"It's a harmless escape. Nobody's getting hurt."

These are some of the first things that may come to your mind if you are someone who indulges in sexual fantasies or masturbates. And while it certainly is "normal" in the sense that almost everyone struggles with this type of sexual sin to some degree, it is *not* harmless.

Ask Christie[1] who just found out that her husband has been looking at pornography on the Internet for months. She feels betrayed, deeply hurt, and wonders how she'll ever trust him again. And she can't help wondering what's wrong with her. If her husband chooses to look at other women, then she must be lacking something.

Ask Robert who realizes now that every minute he spent escaping into his fantasy world was a minute he didn't spend building healthy relationships with his wife and children. He treated them more like inconveniences—interruptions to the life of comfort and ease he wanted—than family. He tuned out the stressful demands of family life and found escape in sexual fantasy and pornography. Now he is estranged from his children, and his marriage is in shambles.

How Sexual Escapes Harm Relationships

To understand how sexual escapes harm your relationships, take a moment to examine your fantasies as more than imaginary movie clips. When we take apart your fantasy world what do we see? First of all, notice this simple fact: your fantasies are about more than sex; they are about *relationships*. That is, sex is more than a physical act; it is something that you do with a person, not an object. Your fantasies are populated with people (some of whom I'll bet you know).

For a moment look beyond the sex acts and explore these fantasy relationships in nonsexual terms. How would you describe their attitudes? How are they relating to you?

Don't just answer, "They are enjoying themselves," or "They are giving me pleasure." Let me ask you to be a little more honest. In most cases people are fawning over you. You are the center of attention in a world where no one cares about anything but you. You are in a world where the people who normally ignore you cannot seem to resist you. You are in a world where people who don't even know you mindlessly turn away from marital fidelity and all other moral and social norms to be with you.

Am I getting close? Perhaps your fantasies take an even darker turn. Maybe your fantasies aren't about being liked at all, but about power and control. Your fantasies become a playground for anger and frustration, and you enjoy the thought of degrading others or making them cringe before you.

Playing God with Other People

In the secret places of your mind, where you have free reign to live in a world with the kinds of relationships you desire most, what do your relationships look like? In relational terms, sexual fantasies are a world where you practice selfishness and manipulation. Would you honestly describe any of this as love? No matter how widely your fantasies may vary, in every instance you play god with people. You reduce those made in the image of the true God to mindless robots who serve your whims.

"OK, so I'm a selfish uncaring person in my fantasies. So who's being hurt?" you might ask. But remember Robert? His sexual escapes hurt himself and others because his relationships were negatively affected. You may not have noticed it yet, but the way you practice relationships in your heart will not stay safely contained. The violations of love that become the habit of your mind will inevitably find their way into the real world. That habit will contaminate all of your relationships, and in all likelihood it already has.

That doesn't mean you will have an affair, molest children, or become a rapist, though sexual fantasy can certainly fuel those temptations. What's more likely is that the same self-focus, pleasure seeking, and escapist attitudes that rule your sexual fantasies will infect your marriage and friendships.

Rather than learning to work through the tough moments of relationships, you will become more and more likely to seek momentary escapes. Daily irritations become reasons to tune out others and visit the secret world you've created in your mind. Perhaps, without realizing it, you will begin to export the habits of your lust (comfort, convenience, pleasure on demand, etc.) into the real world.

A Biblical Warning

We shouldn't be surprised then that the Bible warns us about making overly neat distinctions between what happens in our minds or hearts and what happens in our lives. In Matthew 5:27–28 Jesus warns, "You have heard that it was said, 'Do not commit adultery.' But I tell you that anyone who looks at a woman lustfully has already committed adultery with her in his heart." Jesus knows that we often take dangerous comfort in believing that the hidden sins of the heart are harmless.

Similarly, Proverbs 27:19 tells us, "As water

reflects a face, so a man's heart reflects the man." In other words, the activities of your heart—your fantasies—reflect truths about you as a person. Do you like what your fantasies reveal about you?

In your heart you are creating a world that is completely opposed to God and his love. God does not treat people as objects to be manipulated and used, but values them and cares for them. God cares about what you are doing and who you are becoming in your heart.

Jesus Came to Free Us

Jesus didn't come just to police our sexual lust, but to free us from it. He is able to help because he has experienced all of the temptations that drive sexual lust and overcome them. He knows the temptation to escape hardship, to be served by others rather than serve them, to want pleasure rather than face difficulty. The Bible describes Jesus this way, "[Jesus,] being in very nature God, did not consider equality with God something to be grasped, but made himself nothing, taking the very nature of a servant, being made in human likeness . . . he humbled himself and became obedient to death—even death on a cross!" (Philippians 2:6–8). Jesus knew what it is like to be God himself! He could do everything the easy way, never inconveniencing himself one bit. But instead, he came to this broken world and served us, doing what was necessary to cleanse and forgive us. He did all that so he could be in relationship with us. And it cost him a painful, agonizing death. Out of love for his heavenly Father and for us, he chose the path of service and love rather than escape and comfort. Jesus wants us to know his love, and he wants to give us the power to overcome temptation.

You may not believe it, but the truth is that Jesus' love is far sweeter than any world of self-indulgence you can create. If you haven't already realized it, you will: your fantasy world is an empty world of phantoms and darkness that will only make you miserable in the long run.

What Feels Like Death Brings Life and Joy

Choosing to say no to lust and yes to love isn't easy. Saying no to something that seems to have offered comfort and pleasure can feel like dying. It seems contradictory, but the truth is, being willing to go through the suffering of saying no to yourself and saying yes to the challenges of real love leads to life and joy. Jesus put it this way: "I tell you the truth, unless a kernel of wheat falls to the ground and dies, it remains only a single seed. But if it dies, it produces many seeds. The man who loves his life will lose it, while the man who hates his life in this world will keep it for eternal life" (John 12:24–25).

When a seed falls to the ground and begins to grow, in a sense, the seed is destroyed. But, really, the seed is just becoming what it was always made to be—a mature, productive plant. You weren't made for selfishness. You were made to love as God loves you, and that means doing the hard work of relationships at the cost of your own comfort.

When you love others the way God loves you, your relationships will be characterized by real, lasting love, not phony, escapist lust that lasts a moment and ruins lives. You can't do this for yourself, but Jesus can do this in you. He promises us in 2 Peter 1:3 that "his divine power has given us everything we need for life and godliness," and Jesus keeps all of his promises.

Practical Strategies for Change

Would you like to build a new inner world founded on Christ's love? Here are a few steps to get you started.

Steps to Building a New Inner World

Start by confessing to God that you have created a world that is opposed to his love. Ask him for forgiveness right now. You will need God's forgiveness and love every day as you turn away from your fantasy world. Habits die hard, especially ones that deliver the kind of excitement and immediate rush that sexual lust does. You won't simply have to say no just once, but many times, and sometimes you will fail. It's important for you to understand that no matter how many times you fail and no matter how long this battle lasts, you cannot exhaust God's love and forgiveness. The Bible says, "If we claim to be without sin, we deceive ourselves and the truth is not in us. If we confess our sins, he is faithful and just and will forgive us our sins and purify us from all unrighteousness" (1 John 1:8–9). Notice that God's purifying work is based on *his* faithfulness, not yours. Take responsibility for your sin, trusting that God will forgive and cleanse you because of his faithfulness, not yours.

Don't go it alone. Find others who are committed to having pure thoughts and meet with them for encouragement, prayer, and accountability. Your local church is a good place to start. Many Bible-believing churches have support groups and Bible studies that can help. If you aren't already a member of a church, find one that will not just point you to your problems, but to Jesus as the solution. You need to regularly hear about God's love and forgiveness. Find a friend or group, too, that doesn't simply share in your struggle, but reinforces what you hear on Sunday morning. You need relationships that remind you of who you are becoming in Christ, not just who you are as a struggler.

If you are married, be careful how you share your struggle with your spouse. In a Christian marriage, Christ's love and forgiveness should make it safe for us to reveal our sins to each other and receive help and understanding. Who better to help us with our weaknesses than our spouses who know us intimately and have promised to nurture us in love and act in our best interest? However, in asking for your spouse's help and support, you must be careful to not injure him or her.

In most cases you are not engaging in sexual fantasy to intentionally hurt your spouse, but it is a form of betrayal and hurtful to your spouse. In addition to being hurt, knowing too much about a spouse's battle with sexual lust can create terrific fear and insecurity. This, in turn, can lead to overzealous "policing" behavior on the part of the offended spouse. When that happens, daily interrogations and accusations end up creating more secrecy, shame, and marital distress.

How much and how often you should share this struggle depends, in large part, on the health of your marriage. Do you normally share spiritual struggles with each other? Are there other past or current betrayals that will inform your spouse's response? As in all communication, the rule of thumb is "speaking the truth in love" (Ephesians 4:15). Provide truth in a measure and manner that will strengthen the relationship, not damage it.

In my counseling experience, this usually means it is appropriate to share with your spouse that a battle in this area exists and to ask for prayer and encouragement, but it is hurtful to share the content of your fantasies. In general, you should be seeking primary accountability and support from a counselor or other wise friends.

Learning to Love Real People in the Real World

Ask Jesus to teach you how to love others in tangible ways. Replace old habits of escapism and avoidance by learning how to communicate honestly and deal with relational problems directly. Rather than living in a world of selfish pleasures, learn the joys of being with and serving others in love. Christ's love is made complete in you as you share it with others.

The Bible says, "This is love: not that we loved God, but that he loved us and sent his Son as an atoning sacrifice for our sins. Dear friends, since God so loved us, we also ought to love one another. No one has ever seen God; but if we love one another, God lives in us and his love is made complete in us" (1 John 4:10–12). God has shown us perfect love in Christ, so we learn how to love from him. If you want to learn how to love, then become a lifelong student of Jesus.

This isn't just about kicking a bad habit. God promises that, as you live a life of love by trusting in Christ, God's love will become visible through you.

What could be more meaningful than making God's love visible to others? This same passage helps us to see how special that love is: God's love is sacrificial. He puts our needs first even though it costs him a high price. Your basic compass heading for love is to do what is best for others even if it costs you. Your initial sacrifice will be your own comfort and lusts. When you are tempted to escape, look around, notice what others need in that moment and serve them.

What this looks like in a real-life relationship. To help you understand this, let me tell you about a man I counseled named Peter. He was dissatisfied with the frequency of sexual intimacy in his marriage to Mary; he wanted to make love more often than she did. He dealt with this relationship problem by fantasizing about Mary and masturbating. He believed that because he was thinking about Mary, what he was doing was okay.

But what would real, sacrificial love for his wife look like in this situation? There are many possibilities, but you can be sure that it does NOT look like being alone in a room having sex by himself. This doesn't communicate love to his wife; it communicates love for himself. This behavior takes the God-given meaning out of sex and turns it into a form of self-medication. This might seem harmless, but in the long run, Peter's lack of love towards Mary creates more problems.

What are some of those problems? Inevitably he will be creating more and more dissatisfaction with his real wife, because no matter how attentive she might be, she will not be able to match the creativity and convenience of the fantasy wife his imagination has created. Certainly it is also likely that Mary will not remain the object of Peter's fantasies for long because his imagination will require more and more novelty to fuel sexual excitement.

But even worse, the convenience of only having to please himself will inevitably keep him from doing the hard work of creating real intimacy by spending time in conversation and problem solving. Peter's solution to his problem will only make him more self-centered and will erode his marriage. But what if, instead of thinking about how to satisfy himself and his needs, he sought to expand his understanding of how to love Mary and found ways to express that love concretely? Then, instead of being isolated and alone, he would be building a real relationship of love with her that would reflect Christ's love.

How about you? Who are the real people that God is calling you to love and build a relationship with? Instead of focusing on your fantasies and sexual satisfaction, look around at all the real people God has put into your life for you to love and serve. There is an almost infinite variety of ways to express love to others; many of them, believe it or not, are quite exciting. Ask God to stretch your understanding of love. Think about how you can love sacrificially those who are in your life. Instead of treating the people in your life as objects in your sexual fantasies, think of them as your brothers and sisters in the Lord. Ask God to help you know how to love and serve them. As you do so your life will grow richer in real relationships, and your fantasies will pale by comparison.

Replacing your old habits of sexual fantasy with new habits of repentance, accountability, and sacrificial love will not be easy. But remember, every time you fall in this area, you have "one who speaks to the Father in [your] defense—Jesus Christ" (1 John 2:1). Remember also that Jesus has not left you alone. He has given you the gift of the Holy Spirit, and "the one who is in you is greater than the one who is in the world" (1 John 4:4). Like all spiritual struggles, we overcome as we learn to rely on the Spirit and daily ask him to change us to be like Christ.

Endnotes

1. All names in this booklet are fictitious and personal details have been changed.

Simple, Quick, Biblical

Advice on Complicated Counseling Issues
for Pastors, Counselors, and Individuals

MINIBOOK
CATEGORIES

- Personal Change
- Marriage & Parenting
- Medical & Psychiatric Issues
- Women's Issues
- Singles
- Military